Michael Rawson

2002

LINCOLNSHIRE MEMORIES

DAVID CUPPLEDITCH

SUTTON PUBLISHING

First published in the United Kingdom in 1998 by
Sutton Publishing Limited · Phoenix Mill
Thrupp · Stroud · Gloucestershire · GL5 2BU

British Library Cataloguing in Publication Data
A catalogue record for this book is available from the British Library

ISBN 0 7509 2014 9

TM ALAN SUTTON™ and SUTTON™ are the
trade marks of Sutton Publishing Limited

Typeset in 11/15 pt Baskerville.
Typesetting and origination by
Sutton Publishing Limited
Printed in Great Britain by
WBC Limited, Bridgend.

Many members of the South Wold Hunt bought their horses at fairs. The hounds were kennelled at Edlington, a small village just north of Horncastle.

CONTENTS

Joseph Willey (1829–93), the Victorian photographer, giving his two children a few pointers about gardening.

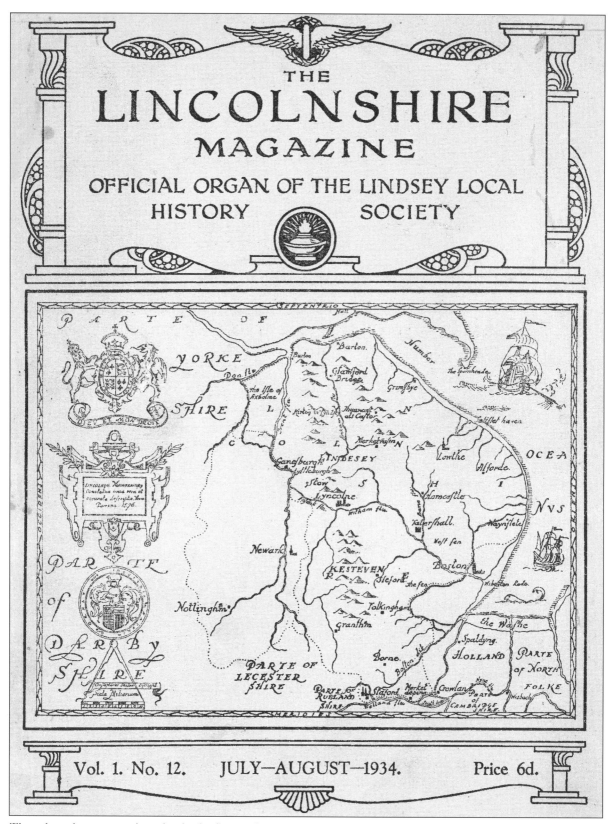

THE

LINCOLNSHIRE

MAGAZINE

OFFICIAL ORGAN OF THE LINDSEY LOCAL HISTORY SOCIETY

Vol. 1. No. 12.   JULY—AUGUST—1934.   Price 6d.

There have been magazines, books, leaflets and, more recently, videos recording Lincolnshire's illustrious history over the years, none better than *The Lincolnshire Magazine*, which was a cross between the factual dourness of Lincoln Society Records and the light-hearted coffee-table appeal of *Lincolnshire Life*.

INTRODUCTION

Because community life is constantly changing, and not necessarily for the better, nostalgia has become fashionable rather like a tonic. In some cases people like to reflect on a time when life was hard but fair, although many now view bygone times through rose-tinted glasses; in other cases people try to look back to see why our so-called intelligent and sensible society has gone so horribly wrong. Both these reasons mirror an unhappy and dissatisfied nation. One of the reasons that society has got itself into such a tangle is the mass of bureaucratic red tape which everyone needs just to complete the simplest of jobs. Another is uncertainty for the future and scepticism in the workplace which, coupled with competition (an area that has got totally out of control), has almost destroyed traditional English values and certainly turned them upside down. In the role of the sexes too there is deep confusion and to cap everything else the threat of automation lies over everybody's head, and can put the most loyal of employees out of work in an instant.

Lincolnshire is fairly fortunate, like Northumberland, because it is not *en route* to anywhere else. There is no passing traffic and so it has remained, as it always was, isolated and alone despite one or two emigrés who have brought with them their 'rat race' mentality. There used to be an old unwritten law in Lincolnshire that a family had to live in a town or village for forty years before they were accepted. Pedantic it might have been, but it saved the community which has been put to test in recent times.

Over the past thousand years the same family names occur in Lincolnshire records time and time again. The Heneages, Tyrwhitts, Dymokes, Sibthorpes, Pelhams, Neviles, Thorolds and Cracrofts crop up frequently, while in the south of the county the Cecils, Brownlows and Ayscoughs still keep appearing. Several other names, such as the Coneys, Welbys, Tunnards, Willoughbys, Freshneys and Tilneys ought to be mentioned, while the D'Isneys of Norton Disney eventually spawned that famous American patriarch of the entertainment world, Walt Disney.*

Lincolnshire has also produced some enterprising sons and daughters over the years in other fields, from explorers – Matthew Flinders, John Franklin and Captain John Smith (Admiral of New England and a Governor of Virginia) – to Christian denizens, such as John Wesley, Charles Wesley and John Whitgift, Archbishop of Canterbury at the time of Elizabeth I. There have been sportsmen like Geoff Capes, Tony Jacklin and Mary Cheetham (hockey) and people in the entertainment world, like Nicholas Parsons, Arthur Lucan ('Old Mother Riley'), Patrick Wymark and Freddie Frinton, and politicians, like Margaret Thatcher and Norman Lamont. In the military field there have been field marshals such as Sir William Robertson (1860–1934) of Welbourn, the first private in the British Army to attain the rank of Field Marshal, the Bromheads of Thurlby and Sir Archibald Massingberd of Gunby, while numerous artists have found inspiration in the county. Peter de Wint often sketched and painted around the Lincoln area and George

Stubbs rented a desolate farmhouse near Barton-on-Humber to complete some sketches for his *Anatomy of the Horse* published in 1766. Alfred Lord Tennyson, the Victorian Poet Laureate, was born in Somersby, Sir Isaac Newton, father of the law of gravity, came from Woolsthorpe and the botanist Sir Joseph Banks lived at Revesby.

There are examples by many Lincolnshire photographers in this book, although the one omission is Frank Parkinson, the Spalding photographer who specialised in photographing dead children's corpses. Of all the hundreds (possibly even thousands) of photographs that I looked at to make a selection for this book, the one photograph that haunts me is Frank Parkinson's self-portrait with family and dead child in a coffin. This was Edwardian sentimentality gone mad. Some photographs are for public use and celebrate events, happenings, episodes or experiences but this particular photograph revolted me; how could someone exhibit such a tragic and intimate scene of private grief and put it on public display.

It would have been very easy to fill this book with images of Burghley House, Belton House, Doddington Hall, Frampton Hall, Fillingham Castle, Grimsthorpe Castle, Harlaxton Manor, Aubourn, Gunby and the like. But it would have left little space for anything else and Lincolnshire is a very big county, as many historians have discovered. Instead I have tried to give a small cross-section of the other side of life in Lincolnshire, quite apart from these rambling great houses, magnificent though they may be, complete with quirks and foibles, and if by chance there are any errors I humbly apologise.

* The Disney family from Isney, near Caen, came over to England with the Norman conquerors and were given the manor of Norton Disney in 1067. The family estates were sold to Christopher Monk, the Duke of Albemarle, in 1674 after the eldest son had joined the Duke of Monmouth's forces and was hanged by the famous Judge Jeffreys. The Disneys then moved to Ireland. Two hundred years later one branch of the family moved back to Lincolnshire while another moved to America. Walt Disney was descended from the American branch and he visited Norton Disney with his wife and two daughters in 1949, possibly to trace his family tree.

It was the pony and trap which offered the most dependable service. Mrs Sarah Harley (a village midwife for over fifty years) used a pony and trap for her return journey from Bicker to Donnington Market.

SOME LINCOLNSHIRE PHOTOGRAPHERS

Vanity demanded that Edwardian ladies should have their photograph taken. It offered the chance to show off their finest dresses, wear their finest jewellery and pose in the latest hairstyles. This portrait was by Walter Smith of The Studio, Station Road, Spalding.

The girl in this portrait is Helen Gosling. She sent this photograph to her friends and relatives at Christmas time instead of a Christmas card. The photograph was by A. Blades of Queen Street, Horncastle.

Children often made useful appendages, as can be seen in this family group taken by J.S. Bullen of Grimsby. The subject is Mrs G. Hall with her two young daughters, Mary and Freda. There will be many attics throughout Lincolnshire where photographs of this sort are gathering dust.

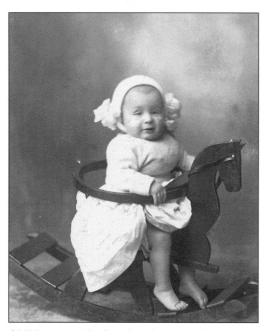

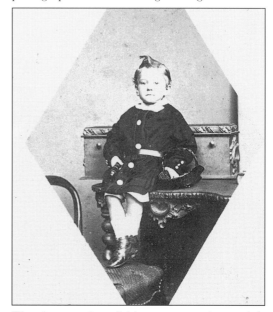

Children could often be photographed as the main subject, as can be seen in this example of 14 February 1911 by J. Spencer Baldry, the Lincoln photographer.

The photographer of this most unusual portrait is unknown. The poor child, leaning against a chest of some sort, has endured a liberal sprinkling of Brylcreem, or the Victorian equivalent, on its hair.

One of the finest portrait photographers to capture young Victorian and Edwardian mademoiselles on camera was George Hadley of 36 Castle Hill, Lincoln. Some of his photographs are as fresh today as the day they were taken. His Victorian portraits are also more informal than the stiff predictable poses usually associated with that age. This photograph of one of the Cottingham sisters, aged sixteen, was taken in 1892.

In this other Hadley portrait, also taken in 1892, of the other Cottingham sister, the photographer has asked the sitter to look to one side. The result is a charming study showing all the frills of Victoriana, captured in the twinkling of a photographer's eye.

This Slingsby portrait which was taken a few years earlier has a much more stilted look about it in comparison. There is a dullness in the sitter's face which conveys sadness. Robert Slingsby's studio at 168 High Street was taken over by Harrison in 1896.

Another early Victorian photographer was W. Audas of 28 Freeman Street, Grimsby. This typical pose of an ecclesiastical gentleman sporting watch, chain and fob also has that Victorian stiffness about it. The pose looks artificial, almost as if the photographer had said: 'Now come on, you've got to look serious as befits a man of the cloth.'

A later Grimsby photographer, J. Browne of 37 Victoria Street, was probably more sympathetic to his sitter. This pose is much more casual. Browne took over T.K. Wardle's successful business.

Working at about the same time as J. Browne in Grimsby was Arthur James of Louth. His *carte-de-visite* shows many similar traits to the previous portrait.

Photographer Oliver Burdett was also based in Louth at 120 Eastgate. This charming portrait study, *c.* 1890, was typical of the Victorian period – a gent in a frock coat.

Another Louth portrait photographer was Clarence James of Alexandra Studio at 1 Ramsgate, Louth, who may have picked up some tips from George Hadley of Lincoln.

In this further portrait by Clarence James, of a young soldier of the 1st Lincolnshire Rifle Volunteers holding his Lee-Metford rifle, the shooting cup which he has won is proudly on display.

H. Warren was a photographer at Queen Street, Market Rasen, and also appears at Barnetby-le-Wold.

This young swell, photographed by Clarence James, is complete with watch-chain, fob and walking cane.

This portrait of an old Victorian lady in her dowager years and probably reading her Bible was taken in the garden. Perhaps she was too infirm to travel to A. Whitehead's studio at Goxhill?

Although most photographers in the Victorian and Edwardian era were men, the prolific Mrs E. Higgins of Stamford showed that sex did not matter. She established her photography business in early 1854. (The first photograph ever was taken in 1849.) This example shows that she possessed a keen eye.

When T.K. Wardle of Riverhead, Grimsby, started his career he chose the Grimsby arms for his logo, yet, when he moved to 34 Victoria Street West, his logo had changed to a brigantine battling its way through rough seas. Was he reprimanded for his original choice?

Just as Grimsby was awash with fish at the turn of the century and prosperity followed, so it was with photographers. This was a portrait by W. Brumpton, who was a gold medallist, of 7 Crescent Street, Grimsby.

The Lowthian brothers were based at 144 and 146 Freeman Street. This delightful family group was photographed in the Lowthian Art Studio, with father leaning against that famous prop which was to appear in so many of their photographs.

In this further Lowthian portrait study the same prop appears! The brothers seem to have acquired commissions from the prosperous middle classes.

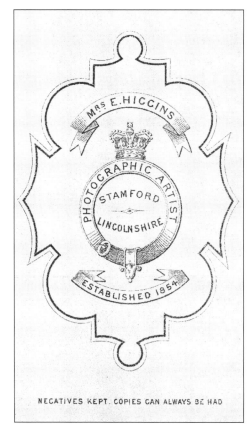

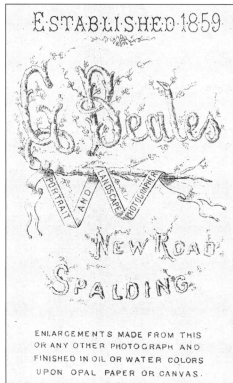

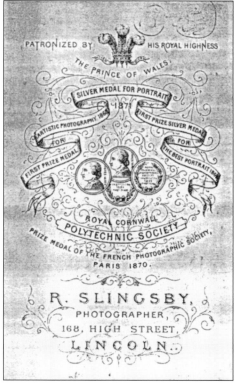

Quite often the backs of *cartes-de-visite* can be just as informative as the fronts. This selection by Mrs E. Higgins (Stamford), B. Duckmanton (Gainsborough), G. Beales (Spalding) and R. Slingsby (Lincoln) shows that Lincolnshire cashed in on the photography craze in its infancy.

This delightful study of a young child sitting on an animal skin was captured by photographer H. Jancowski of 3 Market Place, Grimsby, who also had premises in Eastgate, Louth.

Some children made better sitters than others. This was one of Wardle's portraits and, despite making the sitter feel at ease in a comfortable armchair with her favourite doll, she was still not going to smile.

In this sympathetic Jenkins and Remy portrait of a young girl there is a wonderfully classical air, reminiscent of a pre-Raphaelite pose.

This was a typical portrait by the Alford studio, Nainby. Nainby's chief opposition was the firm of Plumtree & Smith which was also based in Alford.

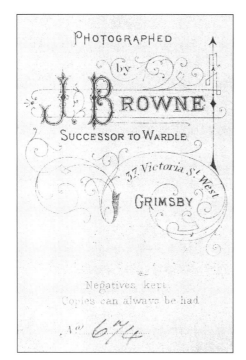
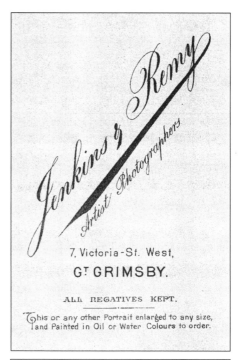
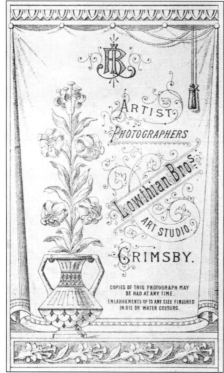

The wealth that Grimsby and Cleethorpes enjoyed from the fishing industry meant that there was no shortage of photographers: T.K. Wardle (Riverhead and Victoria Street), the Lowthian brothers (144/146 Victoria Street), J. Browne (37 Victoria Street), Jenkins and Remy (7 Victoria Street), W. Audas (42 Freeman Street), W. Brumpton (7 Crescent Street), S. Burton (Cleethorpe Road), J.S. Bullen (183 Freeman Street), H. Dawes (42 Freeman Street), Edwin Noble (233 Freeman Street), W.M. Marsden (3 Market Place), H. Jancowski (3 Market Place), G.H. Greenwood (36 Hainton Street), W. Garthwaite of 187 Cleethorpe Road, G.W. Von Dix, also of Cleethorpe Road, and Alfred Clark of Cleethorpes. These are four examples of the backs of Grimbarian *cartes-de-visite*.

A particularly striking design can be found on the back of W. Audas' cabinet portrait cards. Depicting two cherubs and what looks to be a masonic symbol over his initials, Audas proudly boasted of the patronage of the Duke and Duchess of Connaught, HRH Prince Albert Victor, the Earl of Yarborough and Lady Yarborough, the Earl of Ellesmere, Lady Eleanor Heneage and Mr Heneage MP. Quite a clientele!

This was one of Caleb Smith's portraits, taken in 1892 when the sitter, James M. Goy, was nineteen years old. Caleb Smith divided his time between 1 Norman Place, Lincoln and 39 Wide Bargate, Boston.

John Starbuck, the photographer of East End, Alford, paved the way for Edwin Nainby, a later Alford photographer who achieved much acclaim for his seaside studies and informal family groups. This was one of Nainby's studio portraits.

This portrait of Edwin Nainby and his wife, Jane, shows why he was so well remembered. His face portrays a man with a sense of humour. Born in 1842, Edwin Nainby worked with John Starbuck and they became partners, Edwin eventually marrying John's daughter, Jane.

Edwin Nainby and his daughter, Ada, about to set off on a photographic commission. His camera and photographic aids were kept in the rear of the trap.

G. Beales of New Road, Spalding, was another early photographer working in the county. He established his business in 1859, only five years after Miss Higgins of Stamford. This was one of his *carte-de-visite* portraits. The name also appears in Boston under F. Beales of 31 High Street, later known as F. & G. Beales Borough Studio of 31 High Street and 2 West Street, Boston.

Of all the portraits this one of a young girl taken by W.M. Marsden in Grimsby must rank as my favourite. It possesses all the qualities of a young Edwardian woman on the threshold of life, wrapped in her fur stole.

Sometimes the photographers' names on the backs of these photographs would be filled with medals boasting previous photographic achievements won at various competitions. Sometimes they would just be certificates. Occasionally the photographer's name and logo, such as F. Westoby of Epworth and Crowle, Edwin Nainby of Alford and Spilsby or W.P. Carlton of Horncastle, was sufficient.

Even Joseph Matthews' advert is acceptable. It is not too flowery but to the point. Joseph Matthews succeeded Clarence James in his photographic business and saw himself as a failed artist turned photographer. However, it has often puzzled me why no one has compiled a compendium of Lincolnshire photographers. There have been books on nearly every other local subject in recent years, and why photographers have been omitted is a complete mystery. It would certainly sort out the puzzle of who was Signor Luigi Cella of 7 Wide Bargate, Boston, who was C. Fieldhouse of Market Rasen and who was Mrs S.F. Clarke (the dentist's wife) of 8 Upgate, Louth.

Most Victorian families liked to be seen as a close-knit group, such as this one photographed in the studio of Joseph Willey of Louth, *c.* 1870. But look at the expression on the aunt's face: she is the one standing in the background.

The other image which the Victorians, and especially the Edwardians, liked to portray was the 'out-of-doors' look. This was a family outing photographed near Ludborough. All the Edwardian ladies are sporting their best bonnets and hats in an age when the afternoon ramble was fashionable.

There was nothing Victorians and Edwardians liked better than a good wedding. The photograph of this wedding party was taken at Chapel St Leonards. Note that a carpet has been laid on the front lawn just for the photograph.

Funerals were also held in high regard. Everything was doom and gloom, with the departed mourned 'with a sense of decorum'. Black armbands, shutters closed, flowers in profusion and handkerchiefs at the ready as this group pays its last respects. This was another of Nainby's studies.

By the turn of the century photography had become a universal pastime and was available to almost anyone. Chemists' shops dispensed films and developing facilities the way they dispensed their prescriptions. Everyone had a chance to use these new photographic skills and the family snapshot in the back yard became commonplace. This was one Lincolnshire family photographed at the rear of their home.

At Croxby, a tiny Wold village, the photographer Arthur Stephenson found himself in a bit of a dilemma in about 1930. To take his photograph he had to climb on to the top of this shed. It clearly stated: 'Notice – Any person or persons found damaging this shed or fishing gear will be prosecuted'!

TRANSPORT IN LINCOLNSHIRE

The old days of a flagman walking in front of a train to warn people off the track has long since disappeared. This photograph of a flagman was taken in about 1929 at Bourne, not far from the GNR station of Red Hall.

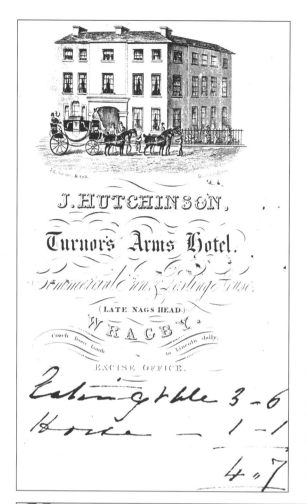

In the days before photography was invented, when coaches and horses were the only form of transport, elaborate bill-heads were produced – such as this one for J. Hutchinson, proprietor of the Turnor's Arms Hotel in Wragby (formerly the Nag's Head) and in the early 1800s an Excise Office. It has recently been returned to its former glory by Hugh Bourne, the Wragby property developer.

Wragby is a reminder of those once commonplace sheep and cattle fairs, which were held four times a year in the Market Square. The name of Wragby (together with a number of other Lincolnshire place names) crops up in the novels of D.H. Lawrence.

Of all the coaches and carts that were made in Lincolnshire (and there were many) this must rank as one of the most unusual. The passenger who rode on this trap from Grimsby to Hull said: 'the boy (the jockey on the horse) drives you just as he is on the postcard.'

The rulley in this photograph by S. Burton of Cleethorpe Road was used to transport fish crates. This is Murray Street on the Grimsby Fish Docks, with the railway line on the left being part of the Cleethorpes to Dock station branch. The building in the background was (for a time) the offices of the North Eastern Steam Fishing Co. Ltd.

Before the First World War there was plenty of work for shire horses and cart horses on the various estates in Lincolnshire. This is George Vickers (groom) proudly showing off his prize shire horse in 1915 at Binbrook Manor.

Although it must be difficult for the present generation to imagine, the Horse Fair was once an intrinsic part of Lincolnshire's calendar. This is the famous Horncastle Horse Fair, which was the biggest horse fair in England in the nineteenth century. This view of it from South Bridge and Waterside was taken by Herbert Carlton, photographer, of 8 High Street Horncastle and Woodhall Spa.

This is the Lincoln Horse Fair, which took place in High Street and occasionally spilled over into St Mary's Street.

Old habits die hard, and even in the '50s when motorised Land-Rovers and Jeeps were available some farmers preferred to tour their estates on horseback. This is George Hallgath on a round of his farm at Driby Manor.

Of course the railway network made a big difference to Lincolnshire. In the last century it was reliable, it brought employment and it was cost effective.

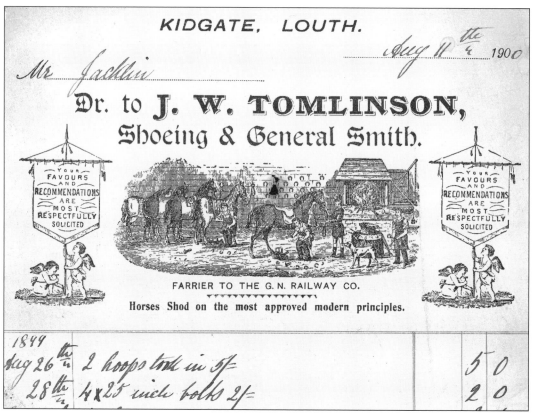

Railway companies often worked in conjunction with farriers and horse-drawn taxis. After all, the train could complete a trek which the horse could not, but the horse could finish off that journey by taking the passenger to his or her front door. These two modes of transport complemented each other for well over a hundred years. It was the advent of the motor car that eventually killed off horse-drawn traffic.

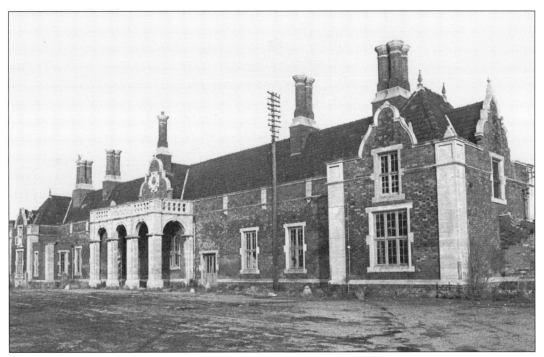

Tomlinson's operation was compatible with the GNR network. They offered their services through one of the finest examples of Tudor Gothic architecture in Lincolnshire, namely Louth railway station, built in 1854. Although it is no longer in use as a station and is perhaps difficult to see, being incorporated into part of a modern housing estate, the building still exists despite desperate attempts by a local property developer to pull it down.

The only station that could match Louth station in architectural elegance was Brocklesby, near Ulceby Junction, although Brocklesby was on a much smaller scale. Edward H. Pennington was the stationmaster at the turn of the century. Brocklesby station, like Louth, is now closed.

All sorts of other trades worked in conjunction with the railway timetable. Here we see some milk churns waiting for the train at Ludborough on the Louth to Grimsby line.

The railway brought with it jobs for footplate men, stationmasters, clerks, inspectors and gatehouse keepers. This is the gatehouse keeper and his family at Well, near Alford, *c.* 1935. Not far from this spot lay a discarded plague-stone under a weeping ash tree on the lawn of the old Manor House at Tothby. It was used in the time of the plague to exchange money for food. The stone contained two cylindrical holes which were filled with vinegar (the nearest thing to disinfectant at that time) into which plague victims could drop their money.

Inevitably there were accidents, such as the Grantham railway disaster of 19 September 1906. Innumerable photographs of this sad event were taken at the time, of which this is just one (published by W.R.C. Wheeler, Bon Marché, Grantham). One of the twelve passengers who were killed, together with engine crew and a GPO sorter, was director of the railway company, a Mr Roland Phillipson, who had just taken his eldest son to school at Eton and was returning to witness the launch of the liner *Mauritania* the next day.

The end of the railway era in Lincolnshire as most of us knew it was a post-Second World War phenomenon, comprising of squabbles between management and unions in British Rail and apathy and shortsightedness on the part of the general public. The Beeching cuts left lines to Grimsby, Lincoln, Grantham and Boston, all of which circumnavigated the county – but left nothing in the middle.

Woodcutting on the South Ormsby estate meant that a traction engine had to be brought on to the scene to drive the woodcutting saw. From left to right are Charlie Dods, Walter Calvert, Hugh Calvert, Jesse Grant, engine driver William Brumpton of Swaby and 'Peg Leg' Willoughby, who owned the donkey.

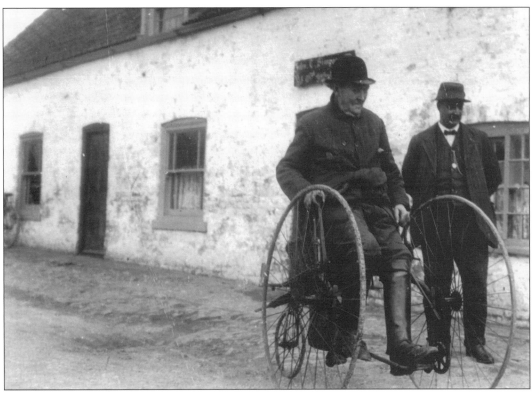

There were several other modes of transport, including this tricycle used at Brant Broughton. Mr Green (a correspondent from the *Gazette*) is on the extreme right, while Mr Woolpit of Brant Broughton is riding the tricycle.

As cycling became popular so clubs sprang up. It was a form of exercise, fun and affordable to most. This is one such cycle club on its outing to Eagle (a village about 8 miles west-south-west of Lincoln). They were photographed outside The Struggler Inn.

Other pubs and hostelries welcomed cyclists and their parties, such as The Ship at Barnoldby-le-Beck.

The cycle craze was to seep through Lincolnshire and probably prompted the formation of a cycle museum in Lincoln. Sadly, about four years ago the marvellous collection, which included every type of machine from the pennyfarthing to Raleigh, was moved to Sheffield and then on to Wales.

When a group of local schoolchildren went on their Sunday School outing at Friskney, near Boston, in about 1905, the trap was replaced with a cart.

Farmers stuck to their old horse-drawn wagons and drays, which had served them well over the years. Besides, most farmers were reluctant to change. The new-fangled motor vehicle might be all right in the city but farmers viewed it with scepticism. This overloaded hay wagon was photographed outside Cuxwold Church in about 1920. The man in front was called West.

Horses gave employment to the hundreds of blacksmiths throughout the county. And *no* farmer wanted to incur the wrath of the village blacksmith, who was already noted for his volatile behaviour. This is the village blacksmith's in Grimoldby.

The Tealby Express, photographed in about 1910 on Temple Terrace, did its best to rival those charabancs of the 1920s and 1930s but it remained the vehicle that it was – a wagonette for passengers between Tealby and Market Rasen. It was a Mr Butters at the reins when this photograph was taken; he was a well-known local personality. Note the one-legged character at the rear of the vehicle.

During the typhoid epidemic of 1904–5 in Lincoln the ambulance-cum-hearse was horse-drawn.

Probably the oddest form of transport in the 1930s was this set of oxen pulling a cart in Caistor. Even in 1935, when this photograph was taken, it looked peculiar – more like 1835 than 1935.

Most farmers believed that the horseless carriage was only a fad of the well-off and would be short-lived. This is part of an advertisement designed to tempt them by James Smith's of North Street, Grantham. These were the days of Talbot, Moon, Briton, Stafford and Tamplin cars. The firm of R. Hornsby & Sons Ltd originated in Grantham and was responsible for manufacturing all kinds of engines. It was the firm's amalgamation with Ruston's of Lincoln that produced the first Ruston-Hornsby car.

Here we see the West family of Lincoln in one of their own motor-powered taxis, c. 1908. So embarrassed was Mr West's father that his son should go into the motor trade that he had to use his mother's maiden name of R.M. Wright!

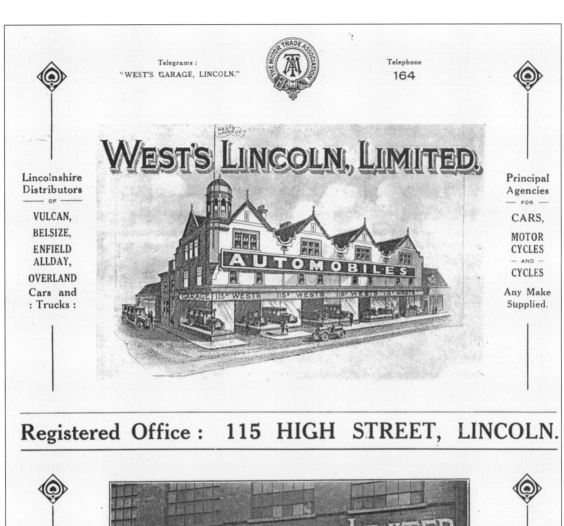

Lincoln, once the hub of industrialisation, came under the influence of the internal combustion engine in the same way as the rest of the country did. West's became probably the biggest distributor of motor-drawn vehicles in the city.

Lincolnshire's history might have taken a very different course had this car succeeded commercially. The Ruston-Hornsby car was first produced in 1920. In the next five years about 1,000 cars were made until production stopped in 1925, when competition from the family car mass-producers became too fierce.

The farmer's lorry took some time to replace the horse and cart. Eventually, in the post-Second World War era, farmers caved in and the lorry became an accepted form of transport, while the Land-Rover with horsebox or carrier cart hitched to the back replaced the horse. This lorry was photographed in Surfleet, near Boston, in 1958.

THE LINCOLNSHIRE
COAST

It was still possible to swim in the North Sea between the wars. However, present-day pollution and dangerous chemicals have curbed that sport and deterred many a potential bather.

In this photograph of the colonnade, Skegness, with the gardens and bowling green in the foreground there is something missing – the Sun Castle had not been built when this picture was taken in about 1932.

This was a lavender seller, pre-First World War, just to remind us of grandma's old wardrobe and chest of drawers smelling of moth balls and lavender. The sign on the front of his stand says 'Who'll buy lavender?'

When the Skegness bathing pool opened in 1928 it was the biggest pool on the east coast – and unheated.

Or there again there was the yachting pool where children could sail their miniature yachts. This was a popular pastime in the '30s and '40s.

Skegness's chief attractions were its beach, golden sands and bracing air!

The popularity of seaside resorts gave rise to a healthy increase in the postcard trade. It became fashionable to send a loved one, friend or relative some small missive. This Skegness postcard has the town crest emblazoned on it.

Tourists flocked to Skegness in their droves. This photograph is of Les Howe (another photographer), with his camera draped over his shoulder (second from right), and family on their outing to Skegness in about 1930.

Not far from Skegness and standing on the hilltop at Burgh-le-Marsh was Hanson's Mill. Built in 1852 on the site of an earlier post-mill, it is now one of Lincolnshire's many redundant windmills and is currently used as a private residence. The miller was Millwright Thompson (dressed in a white coat and sitting on the wall – he was father of Jack Thompson of Alford). The other mill at Burgh-le-Marsh, known as 'Dobson's five-sailer', is still operational.

Donkey rides are just as popular today as they were back in the '30s. This donkey is advertising Eastgate Shopping and Entertainment Market, Ingoldmells. The photograph was taken on Ingoldmells beach in the 1980s.

Typical of the many guest houses and small hotels that flourished between the wars was The Grange hotel (complete with '20s balconies), Chapel St Leonards.

In complete contrast, and looking more like a brick-built entrance to a baronial hall, is the Magdalen College School, Wainfleet, founded in 1484 by William Patten, known as William of Waynflete. He became Bishop Waynflete of Winchester and also founded Magdalen College, Oxford. It smacks of Tattershall influence and operated as a school until fairly recently, when Lincolnshire County Council turned it into a branch library; it is currently a museum. (The photograph is by Hugh D. Martineau.)

At Sutton-on-Sea bell tents (remnants from the First World War) and changing huts lined the shore, where families could change with a modicum of decency before braving the waters.

It is the Howe family once again; they have hired a bell tent between Sutton-on-Sea and Mablethorpe. This time the photograph was taken by Les Howe.

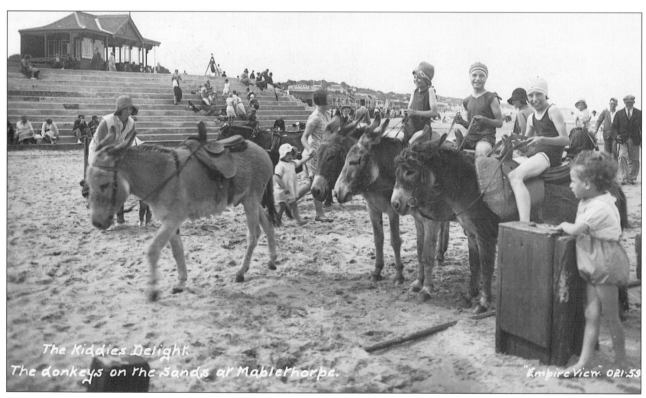

One of the chief attractions along this coast was the donkey rides. This was 'The Kiddies Delight' on the sands at Mablethorpe.

Sutton-on-Sea was something of a refined resort in the '20s. Here we see Mrs Amy Hall and her son Rowland sitting on one of the groynes that led out to sea.

This tranquil view of the paddling pool at Sutton-on-Sea in 1952 was to be shattered the following year when east coast defences were breached in the 1953 floods. This area is now a bowling green and gardens: the present paddling pool (the Maple Leaf) is to the left.

The post office at Trusthorpe is still there neatly tucked away, although the caravan parks, guest houses and holiday complexes are slowly encroaching on its doorstep.

This was a Mablethorpe Group Labour dinner in 1956 with the familiar face of Stan Brumby (second from left).

SMILE, SMILE, SMILE - THAT'S ME!

At Mablethorpe

Mablethorpe was an extremely popular resort in the '20s and '30s largely because of the railway. Its popularity led to a whole spectrum of offshoots, including postcards. This offering was from the 'Jovial' postcard company.

A view of Mablethorpe's central beach in the '50s. The Coastguard lookout is in the far distance and in the centre of the picture some soldiers are combing the beach. All along the shore unexploded bombs were left as a reminder of the Second World War. The Army Bomb Disposal Unit did a wonderful job!

Just as 'Wraite's walking photographs' were a great success in Skegness, so was the Wraite's branch in Mablethorpe. It's that Howe family again – walking towards the beach, this time Marian Howe with son Geoffrey, *c.* 1928.

Photographer F.J. Soar was based in 25 Victoria Road, Mablethorpe, and, if many people associate Mablethorpe with sun, sea and warmth, this is what it looked like in wintertime, *c.* 1956.

The third Mablethorpe photographer was W.W. Camm & Son, of Royal Studios, High Street. This was one of his portrait studies; the young girl is Sally Hall.

A pre-First World War photograph of the Mablethorpe Carnival, or the 'Battle of Flowers' as it was then known.

The two events which capture the public's imagination are the annual 'Carnival' and 'turning on the lights'. Here we see the Mablethorpe lights being turned on by Barbara Windsor, the popular EastEnders actress and past star of those nostalgic 'Carry On' films.

Not far from Mablethorpe is Theddlethorpe All Saints. The Hall is presently owned by the Howell family. It has been occupied by the Carritt, Scrimshaw and Shelbourne families over the years and for a time the roof on this building was tiled. Fortunately its present owners have reinstated the thatch to bring the Hall back to its former glory, as can be seen in this photograph of about 1860.

Many ships have foundered on this treacherous shore. Here we see a two-masted barque that ran aground off Saltfleet in the '20s. It was one of the lucky ones which, fortunately, was refloated on the next high tide.

Shipwrecks and people in difficulty gave local lifeboats plenty of work. There were lifeboats in Skegness, Mablethorpe and Cleethorpes. This lifeboat station was at Donna Nook.

The dominant spire of St Peter's, South Somercotes, became a familiar landmark and an important navigational aid for ships. Unfortunately it was damaged by enemy action in the Second World War, and is currently being repaired by the Churches Conservation Trust.

Even in those heady days of the First World War there was still room for a cup of tea and an afternoon picnic on the beach. This photograph was taken on 2 September 1915 at Grainthorpe.

Ross Castle and Pier.

On the Pier.

Leaking Boot Statue.
Kingsway Gardens.

CLEETHORPES

Kingsway and Gardens.

Storm at Cleethorpes.

On the northern tip of the Lincolnshire coast is the popular seaside resort of Cleethorpes. Once again a plethora of postcards were produced to promote this resort, of which this was one. In the centre is the Cleethorpes mascot of the 'Boy with the Leaking Boot'.

The Warwick Tower, or Cleethorpes Revolving Observation Tower, was opened on 21 June 1902. It was 150 feet high and passengers were revolved to the top by a circular lift. It had the capacity to carry two hundred people.

A Few Lincolnshire Characters

Tom Dixon, a farm labourer from Brinkhill, *c.* 1905. He probably never left Lincolnshire in his life.

In 1697 Henry Harrison, carpenter, took his small son John (born in 1693), his wife Elizabeth, his carpenter's tools and the family bedding and removed them from Foulby, near Doncaster, to the sleepy Lincolnshire village of Barrow-upon-Humber. Henry Harrison was subsequently appointed Parish Clerk of Barrow, an office he was to hold for thirty years, whereas his son John was credited with the invention of the marine chronometer. John Harrison (1693–1776) spent years trying to claim the £20,000 reward due to him, and is the subject of Dava Sobel's best-selling book *Longitude*, published in 1996 by Fourth Estate.

'His face is weather beaten and conker brown' could easily have applied to this old farming type. Lincolnshire has produced many characters over the years, from the agricultural labourer (they were 'the salt of the earth') to the eccentric squire.

Victorian children were brought up to be seen and not heard! The small girl clutching her dolly in this photograph was Miss Broadley of Louth, whose brother Sir Herbert Broadley was (much later!) to be awarded the Freedom of the town.

Photographed on the Smith farm at South Cockerington was this young swell, dressed in gaiters and starched collar. This photograph reminds me of the 'Lincolnshire Poacher', currently the theme of RAF Cranwell and well known throughout the world, mostly through the film *Tom Brown's Schooldays*. The 'Lincolnshire Poacher' has been adopted by singing quartets, pubs, radio hams and even magazines.

This old couple were photographed outside their humble abode at Donna Nook. They were Mr and Mrs Dobson, who lived near the lifeboat house, currently a farm. Mrs Dobson knew the significance of Pag-Rag Day which was 14 May, the day when those in service were entitled to begin a week's annual leave.

The divide between the lower classes and the wealth which surrounded the Earl of Yarborough, for example, was most marked. Here the entire body of Grimsby Town Council has turned out to meet him. The Earls of Yarborough even had their own waiting room at Brocklesby station.

Some itinerants have just passed through the county, like this pair of strolling Italian musicians. They look like father and daughter, and were photographed at Fiskerton, near Lincoln.

Other people doubled up their livelihoods, like Jimmy Gent of Bassingham, who was a postman-cum-shoemaker – a curious combination.

Cuthbert Bradley was a Folkingham artist, who specialised in painting dogs and horses. He died in 1941 aged seventy-four. This photograph was taken in about 1895.

Bartholomew Harrison of South Willingham, near Market Rasen, was a jovial miller.

The difference in characters has been most marked, and about as diverse as one might expect in such a large county. This humble telegraph boy, attached to the GPO, came from Ludborough, and was photographed in about 1900 by A. James of Louth.

Young Frank Nelstrop's first experience on the back of a horse was when he was little more than two years of age, under the careful guidance of his father, Robert at Branston, near Lincoln.

Joe Willoughby of Calceby was a woodman. He also had a wooden leg!

Despite a seemingly hard life, many Lincolnshire women lived to a ripe old age. Here we see Mrs Clay of Swaby off to market with her load of faggots.

Mrs Traves of Barnoldby-le-Beck (mother of the Barnoldby carrier) appeared to have a spartan existence. Yet she still lived to a great age. Lincolnshire people possessed the advantage of stoic resilience. It is a quality which has baffled many visitors to the county.

Another ancient character remembered to this day, from Heighington, near Lincoln, was Ann Speed, pictured here in about 1900 aged ninety; she died aged 102. She is sitting in front of the three gentlemen and is holding a baby (possibly a granddaughter, great-granddaughter or even great-great-granddaughter). With her is Susan Speed. The photograph was taken at Henry Winn's (right) ninety-fifth birthday party.

Mrs Maria Waites of Croft, near Skegness, reached her century and gathered her family around her for a celebratory photograph in the 1930s. Her family spanned four generations!

Lord Heneage of Hainton Hall is the man standing in the doorway, wearing the straw boater. At this time the Heneages employed some seventy-three staff and tenants, one of whom is the bearded Edward Harrison (a tenant farmer) on the extreme right.

Charles Hardy (founder of the firm Hardy & Collins), who farmed extensively in the Boston area, is seated in the centre of the photograph with his wife, in 1921. Harriet Craven is on one side while Maud Grant is on the other. Back row, left to right, are Lilian Craven, Frank Hardy, Florence Tunnard, George Hardy, Doris Marjason, William Hardy, Ethel Wright, Frederick Hardy, Richard Hardy and Edith Neal.

Hiram Hall was a shoemaker and cobbler from Wootton. For some unknown reason he reminds me of 'Mr Pastry' (of TV fame) or a young John Mills after a visit to the make-up department.

Woodthorpe Johnson Clarke (1856–1916), of Binbrook Manor, was a gentleman farmer and, by all accounts, quite a character.

Mr Bray of Willoughton lost his hand while shooting duck with a short-barrelled gun on a dark night.

It is a wonder there were not more accidents with those old scythes. They were razor sharp and glinted in the sunlight; a row of men would cut through a crop with military precision. These two old locals in the Boston area, Johnny Cole (born 1850) with scythe and Joe Bullivant Cole (born 1844) with pitchfork were brothers from Old Bolingbroke.

An occupation that has disappeared is the old scissor-grinder and knife-sharpener, who used to peddle his trade by bike. This one, by the name of Bird, was photographed at Habrough, near the station.

Wheelwrights too have all but gone. This is Samuel Broadley, wheelwright of Tetney, and his family outside their home in about 1875.

Sir Richard Bernard Body has been an MP for Holland with Boston since 1966. He has achieved the reputation of being an almost independent voice within the Conservative Party, a reputation which Austin Mitchell – MP for Grimsby – has gained within the Labour Party. Sir Richard is a barrister of the Middle Temple.

Montagu Allwood was the 'Carnation King'. He was born at Grange Farm, Ludford, and among his many varieties were 'Mary Allwood', 'Allwood's QQ', 'Robert Allwood' and 'Allwood's Cream'. Probably the best known was 'Robert Allwood', a perpetual flowering carnation. There was even a *Dianthus Allwoodii* named after him by the Royal Horticultural Society. He made so much money out of carnations, claiming to be the largest grower in the world, that he formed his own publishing company called Allwood Bros Ltd, of Haywards Heath, Sussex. It was they who published *Carnations and all Dianthus*, *Carnations for Everyman*, *Third and Fourth Generation* (two volumes of autobiography) and *English Countryside and Gardens*.

The gentleman/author, 'Jack' Yates, co-wrote the *Shell Guide to Lincolnshire* with Henry Thorold. Born on Good Friday 1905 in St Michael's Vicarage, Louth, where his father was vicar, Yates was educated at Radley and Oriel College, Oxford. While at Oxford he struck up friendships with John Betjeman and historian A.J.P. Taylor. This is Les Howe's portrait of him.

The Marquis of Exeter, a celebrated sportsman, was born in 1907 in Stamford and educated at Eton and Cambridge, David George Brownlow Cecil was part of the 1928 British Olympic team. This included Abrahams and Liddell, and was later the subject of the film *Chariots of Fire*. Nigel Havers played the part of David Cecil, who won a gold medal in the 440 yd hurdles.

Other celebrated sportsmen have included Geoff Capes, the Lincolnshire strongman, born in Holbeach but associated more with Stamford where he was a policeman. He is seen here at a summer fête at Stainton-le-Vale.

The Royal Lincolnshire Regiment raised nineteen battalions during the First World War. Of the 20,000 men of all ranks, almost half were casualties – killed, missing, prisoners of war or wounded. Four Victoria Crosses were awarded. Here we see the 5th Lincolns at Luton in 1915.

In the Second World War Lincolnshire also played its part. Every area had its own Home Guard. This 'Look, Duck and Vanish' platoon (as they were nicknamed) came from north Lincolnshire. After the war there was a massive party held in the Albert Hall for all those who served in the Home Guard. They were entertained by Vera Lynn and several other top entertainers.

The author of *Enemy Coast Ahead*, Guy Gibson, who commanded 617 Squadron and who requisitioned the Petwood Hotel, Woodhall Spa, to use as his Officers' Mess, was a well-known hero. His exploits were made into a film *The Dam Busters*. Curiously, the star of that film, Richard Todd, also lives in Lincolnshire – near Grantham.

'Old Mr Greenfield's gardener' at the Petwood Hotel, Woodhall Spa. He was photographed with his unusual horse-drawn lawnmower in 1936 by Hugh Martineau. Incidentally, there are mementoes in the hotel bar from the time that Guy Gibson commandeered the hotel as the Officers' Mess for 617 Squadron.

Even in the post-war era there were constant reminders of mobilisation of troops. This was a march past in Horncastle in 1960, with Reg Archer's fish and chip shop and Perkins newsagents in the background. A few locals have turned out to witness the event.

A ceremony to commemorate 103 Squadron (Bomber Command), at Elsham Wolds, 1989. Throughout the county these memorials serve to remind us just how many RAF personnel lost their lives in their duty to their country.

Every Borough Council had its own town clerk in the days of the old borough system. This is Hugh Roberts (or 'Old Hughie Gas and Gaiters' as he was affectionately known), resplendent in his wig and white gloves in about 1930 at the installation of a new mayor of Louth. 'Old Hughie' was Louth's town clerk for many years. The work that these men once did can be achieved by many hundreds of employees, as district councils have discovered. Not only that, but the councils themselves have increased and seem to be multiplying like rabbits. When the newly formed County of Humberside was abolished, instead of reverting back to the proper authorities, three new councils appeared instead!

Lieutenant Commander Douglas Valder Duff (centre of photograph and proudly sporting his Savage Club tie), of Theddlethorpe Rectory, had a varied service record which included a spell with the 'Black and Tans' and the Palestine police. One of his forbears, a Captain George Duff, was killed at the Battle of Trafalgar aboard HMS *Mars*. Commander Duff wrote numerous books including *Baling with a Teaspoon, On Swallowing the Anchor, Palestine Unveiled, Passage-at-Arms, The Rough with the Smooth, Sea Pie* and *Spunyarn (More True Tales of Heroism and Villainy at Sea)*. His autobiography was entitled *May the Winds Blow*. With him in this photograph taken at the Theddlethorpe Garden Fête in 1955 are his wife, the Revd Mr Swaby (author of *A History of Louth*) and Jim Odling. Commander Duff left the area shortly after his wife died in 1960.

There have been unsung heroes, such as the team of surveyors and engineers who reinforced the East Coast sea defences after the disastrous floods of 1953. The team consisted of, left to right, Walter Chambers, Mr Dowdeswell (who owned the cinema at Sutton-on-Sea), R.V. Lewis (Clerk to the Council), Eddie Baker, Mr Hammond and Eric Jordan.

Happy times at Lincoln Cathedral are reflected in this 1940s photograph of Sub-Dean Arthur Cook, an honest and religious gentleman. He is seen here seated on the left, with Mrs Evans and friends in the Sub-Deanery garden.

Some people just enjoyed the dignity of their office. This was Kenneth Riches, Bishop of Lincoln from 1956 to 1975, photographed in his study. He was a much admired and respected bishop, who is still remembered to this day for his good offices.

The infamous Duelling Deans of Lincoln who, even after years of wrangling, never managed to agree on their differences in the early 1990s. Watching over this cloisters scene is Bishop Robert Hardy (extreme right), while Dean Brandon Jackson is in the centre of the photograph and Sub-Dean Rex Davis is immediately behind him.

The '50s were a time when Britain lay in limbo. Still recovering from the aftermath of the Second World War and waiting for the violent social changes of the '60s under Harold Wilson's government, it was a time when 'Rock and Roll' first appeared – and when these three debutantes attended a Wragby Young Farmers' Ball, in 1955.

Arguably Lincolnshire's most famous son was Sir Isaac Newton (1643–1727), who first observed the law of gravity. His many talents included mathematics, physics, astronomy and philosophy. he was head boy of Grantham Grammar School in 1654. This statue to him was erected in the town.

Dr Malcolm Sargent (1895–1967) was the conductor who for many years increased the popularity of The Last Night of the Proms. He was educated at Stamford School, where other old boys have included Sir Michael Tippett and M.J.K. Smith, the cricketer who captained England. Malcolm Sargent, later Sir Malcolm and known affectionately as 'Flash Harry', is buried in his native Stamford.

Royalty is not a stranger to Lincolnshire. Edward VII struck up a friendship with Henry Chaplin and the pair would often be seen in and around Lincoln at selected establishments. This photograph was taken during the Duke and Duchess of Gloucester's visit to the Ruston Works in Lincoln in 1943.

HRH Prince Charles' official visit to Lincoln on 6 July 1979, when he visited the firm of Ruston's (except by now it was called Ruston-Bucyrus) and inspected restoration work being carried out at Lincoln Cathedral. The Prince frequently visited Lincoln unofficially when he was stationed at RAF Cranwell, which must have been a nightmare for security.

HRH Princess Anne visited the east coast on 15 September 1993 when she attended functions at North Somercotes, Theddlethorpe and Willoughby Riding for the Disabled.

HRH The Duke of Gloucester planted a tree in Alford on 27 June 1996. His mother, the late Duchess of Gloucester, was the first royal to visit the disaster scene on the east coast after the 1953 floods.

THOSE PICTURESQUE WOLDS

'Owd' Lincolnshire was a fascinating and strangely peaceful place. Here we see a young Lincolnshire lass feeding the chickens at Donington-on-Bain, while an older woman (possibly her mother or grandmother) looks on, by the side of the pump.

This misty scene, set in East Ravendale, between Binbrook and Waltham, possesses a timeless quality.

There were many thatched houses in Lincolnshire in the last century; almost all have disappeared. This is Fotherby church, surrounded by a quaint array of cottages and thatched roofs.

Of all the houses on the Wolds, the one that has long intrigued this author is Somersby Grange, next door to Tennyson's birthplace of Somersby Vicarage. It is an austere building, not large in size but with a mystical presence. This photograph captures the very essence of it: remote yet fascinating, beautiful but not grand. Why it was built in this particular location by Vanbrugh (the architect of Blenheim Palace) is a complete mystery.

Not far away is the famous oak tree at Bag Enderby. Local legend has it that John Wesley (the founder of Methodism) preached here and that the Tennyson children used to hang swings from its branches. Sadly the ravages of time have taken their toll.

Alford children always turned out for ceremonial events. This is the support the town enjoyed for a Sunday School outing in about 1905. Crammed on the wall outside St Wilfred's Church, the mass of children looks to include the Boys' Brigade as well as devout Church of England worshippers.

About 3½ miles south of Alford in the village of Claxby St Andrew is Claxby Hall, built in about 1740 by James Bateman as the dower house to Well Vale Hall. Both houses passed by marriage to the Dashwood family and eventually to the Rawnsley family. Above the staircase are the arms of the Chaplain family of Tathwell, whose daughter Anne married James Bateman. From the south aspect there are fine views over the lawns to Welton Woods.

At nearby Bilsby the mill has long since lost its sails, and only the shell remains. This photograph was taken in about 1900. The miller was a Mr Blanchard, seen standing in the doorway of the mill, while his wife is standing in the doorway of the shop and Darky Joe (whoever he was) is standing next to the cart.

Just around the corner in Bilsby is one of the few remaining thatched cottages in Lincolnshire, completely re-thatched by Marcus Davis in Norfolk reed in 1965.

Bilsby Hall Farm was owned by the Ranby family. Here we see harvest time in about 1924. The Ranby boys were Eric and 'Ren', short for Reynold; the latter is holding a gun. Bilsby Hall is currently owned by the Mablethorpe family.

Not far from Bilsby is Claythorpe Mill. It has suffered many fates in recent years, becoming a restaurant and centre for smoked fish, before being transformed into a wildlife centre. The history of Claythorpe Mill is well documented within the mill museum.

This photograph, taken at Driby Grange at the turn of the century, depicts two maids setting table for a shooting party breakfast.

Harrington Hall was rebuilt by Vincent Amcotts in 1678 in brick, with a splendid sundial over the doorway dated 1681. Then the Amcotts inter-married with the Cracroft family, becoming Cracroft-Amcotts, and eventually moved to Hackthorn Hall. This Nainby study of the Hall, from about 1920, was probably taken when Major Jessop occupied it. The Hall was sold at auction in 1927 to Jabez Atkinson, who set about removing the old oak panelling from the house, but it was saved from demolition by the Rawnsley family of Well Vale Estates.

The Cracroft-Amcotts moved to Hackthorn Hall, just north of Lincoln, which was designed by James Lewis in 1792. It has become well known for its grapes, the first vine being expertly brought to the Hall in 1868 by the head gardener, Donald Moore. In the meantime, the Cracroft-Amcotts have re-married and the present Mrs Bridget Cracroft-Eley is Lincolnshire's Lord Lieutenant.

A gathering for the 1911 Coronation celebrations outside Biscathorpe House. Biscathorpe House still exists, together with the pretty little church dedicated to St Helen, which was rebuilt in 1844 at a cost of £1,000. At the turn of the century the Biscathorpe estate was owned by the Kirkham family.

Another old house to survive is Hagworthingham Old Hall, which was photographed in 1975. Unfortunately, some *leylandii* have been planted since then, almost obliterating the view of the Hall. For most of the last century Earl Manvers was Lord of the Manor of Hagworthingham.

Many large country houses have been demolished in this century. One example, which was demolished in about 1972, was Elkington Hall. Originally built in 1841 to an Italianesque design, it was long the home of the Smyth family. William Henry Smyth, who died in 1912, believed in physical exercise and discipline. Here we see him dressed in his overcoat and hat inspecting a group of Louth Volunteers in 1910.

Nearby Welton Manor (Welton-le-Wold), presently the home of the Pike family, has survived the twentieth century. Here, Sophus and his wife Josephine Neilson are leaving the house for an important engagement in the '50s. The creepers have since been removed, as they have on Biscathorpe House. It is only recently that owners of these large country houses have realised that creeping vine, no matter how attractive visually, causes considerable damage to brickwork and rendering.

It is not just large houses that have been ill-fated in the twentieth century. Lincolnshire's windmills and watermills have also been decimated. This is Covenham Mill, built in 1780 and demolished in 1922. There is currently a restaurant of the same name in the village.

St Bartholomew's Church, Covenham, nr Louth

The pretty little church of St Bartholomew in Covenham nearly suffered the same fate. In 1986 the Americans wanted to demolish this church stone by stone, like London Bridge, and re-erect it in the USA. Fortunately this idiotic scheme was scrapped because of much local opposition.

Nor is it just large country houses and windmills that have perished in the twentieth century. Another victim has been the old village shop. As the changing pattern of post-war shopping turns to impersonalised supermarkets and their incredible buying power, the small village shop has suffered. One example to survive is Roberts' Grocery Store in North Thoresby, photographed here in 1956.

At nearby Fulstow, this was the cricket team in 1910 when there appears to have been an over-abundance of players.

A decorated wagon outside Will Phillips' shop in Fulstow.

Will Phillips' shop in Fulstow still exists, although it has changed drastically from when this interior shot was taken in about 1905; it is now known as Fulstow Village Post Office. Advertised are the *Lincolnshire Times* (now defunct) and the *Grimsby News* (now the *Grimsby Evening Telegraph*). About the nearest anyone will get to seeing what these old shops looked like are the re-creations in the Museum of Lincolnshire Life, Burton Road, Lincoln.

Tattershall Castle was also built in the mid-fifteenth century of local brick, mostly from Edlington Moor and Boston. It had been deteriorating ever since the death of its last resident, Francis Clinton, Earl of Lincoln, in 1693. Ownership then passed to the Fortescue family (who never resided in the castle) until 1910, when a nominee of Terah Franklin Hooley, a Nottingham speculator, managed to purchase it. The castle appeared to be fated until George Nathaniel, Marquis Curzon (a former Viceroy and Governor General of India), stepped in and eventually renovated it between 1911 and 1914. On the death of Lord Curzon in March 1925 the castle was bequeathed to the National Trust.

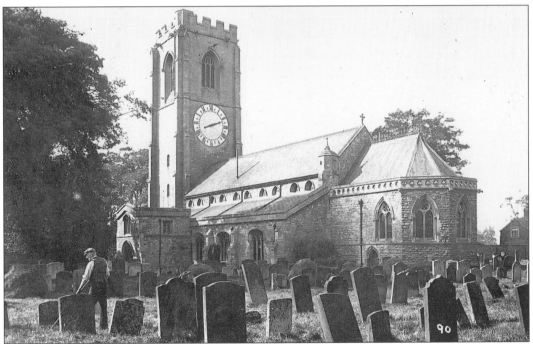

Tattershall's neighbour is Coningsby, lying on the river Bain. Its chief attraction is its church tower clock with a single hour hand. Two eighteenth-century rectors of this church can be found in literary annals. The first was Laurence Eusden, probably the least distinguished poet laureate this country has ever had. According to Thomas Gray, Eusden was an alcoholic cleric who died in Coningsby in 1730. The second, John Dyer (a Welsh lawyer's son), was appointed Rector in 1750, and is chiefly remembered today as an artist-poet.

On the edge of the Wolds is Horncastle. This view of the Market Place in about 1910 has several old Horncastle firms, such as Bryant's, Leggitt's, Maynard's, Salter & Salter and Morton's, surrounding the Stanhope memorial in the centre.

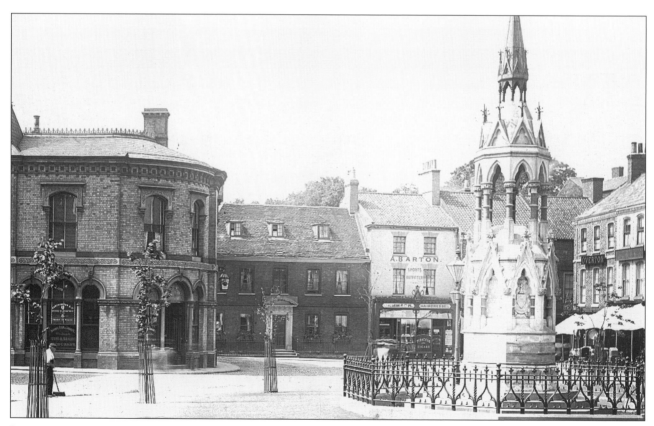

In the opposite direction is the Sellwood family home (centre of photograph), next to the Punch House. Emily Sellwood, daughter of solicitor Henry Sellwood, was to marry Alfred, Lord Tennyson. Sadly the house has been demolished and a Woolworth store erected on the site. The Stanhope memorial, inaugurated in 1899, was in memory of Edward Stanhope, MP for mid-Lincolnshire from 1874 to 1885.

This view of North Street, Horncastle (together with the previous two views) was photographed by Carlton & Sons. In the days before the First World War Horncastle had cobbled streets and was a thriving market town. Recently it has become well known as an antiques centre.

In this view of West Street, Horncastle, *c.* 1900, one can see that businesses and shopkeepers were not frightened to display their wares in the street.

Views of Woodhall Spa.

On the border of the Wolds lies Woodhall Spa. It was the bromo-iodine spring waters that put this place on the map. Victorians and Edwardians flocked to this medicinal watering hole to cure their gout, scurvy and rheumatism. Hotels quickly sprang up to accommodate this fad. Very soon Woodhall Spa became a fashionable retreat resembling parts of Surrey rather than 'owd' Lincolnshire. This group of three Edwardian ladies was taking tea at Woodhall Spa in 1915.

To complement convalescence a little sport was recommended, and what could be better than the gentle game of golf? This was the old golf clubhouse in Woodhall Spa, which has grown somewhat in recent times. The Ladies' Open Golf Championship was played on this course for a number of years and many notable golfing personalities have played a hole or two on these greens.

Subsequently Woodhall Spa became known for its pine-wooded walks, golf and rhododendrons which grew in profusion. The other memorable asset came in the form of a school – St Hugh's Preparatory School, principally for boys, which was started by Ronald Forbes and his wife in 1925. There was a preparatory school in Woodhall Spa before St Hugh's, called Clevedon House Preparatory School, for 'the sons of gentlemen'. This was one of the heats for St Hugh's Sports Day, *c.* 1958. The photograph was taken on the playing fields at the back of the school under the watchful gaze of Sergeant Raw, a First World War veteran and Master of Physical Education.

Thomas Wilson was landlord of the Black Swan, Coningsby (seen here), in 1892; Charles Vinter was landlord of the White Swan. The manor of Coningsby was owned by the Coningsby family, one of whom (Thomas) was created Earl Coningsby, but the family died out in 1729 because there was no male issue. A painting of Coningsby Castle is in existence, though no traces of the edifice now remain.

Between Coningsby and Tumby is a road leading to the Lea Gate Inn, which once served as a beacon to lost travellers before the fens were drained. The name of Lea Gate originates from a former toll. This photograph was taken by Hugh Martineau.

The Lincolnshire Wolds are dotted with charming villages, such as Old Bolingbroke which once had a castle; only the foundation stones remain. King Henry IV was born in this castle, while the church (seen here) was built by John of Gaunt.

Binbrook, where No. 1 Bomber Squadron was based in the Second World War. The broach spire of architect James Fowler's re-creation of Binbrook Church dominates this rural scene.

The pretty village of Tathwell with its lake serves as a reminder that this is the source of the River Lud. Barbara Dickson, the singer-turned-actress, has made her home here.

This is a tranquil picture of the Manor House, Burwell, so typical of many Lincolnshire farmhouses.

Probably the most significant landmark in the postwar era, apart from the Humber Bridge, has been the Belmont mast, near Benniworth. The television transmitter was built in 1965 to a height of 1,265 ft and it dominates the northern part of the Wolds.

It could be an idyllic countryside view of almost anywhere – except that it is Scamblesby in about 1905. At the end of the lane lies the church of St Martin with a tablet to the memory of Mrs Frances Thorndike. In 1672 the Revd Herbert Thorndike (Prebendary of Westminster) gave all his land in Scamblesby, totalling some 378 acres, to the Dean and Chapter of Lincoln to hold in trust.

The back of the Green Dragon pub, West Ashby, *c.* 1870. William Surr, the landlord, stands second from left, wearing a hat and holding a pipe. The pub was left to William Surr's sister, Betsy, who married a Mr Charles Nundy. Charles Nundy died in 1881, which is why Betsy was the landlady in 1895. She died at Kirkby-on-Bain in 1898. The tower of All Saints' Church, visible in the background, was restored in 1871 at a cost of £325 as a memorial to Mrs Barnard, better known as the composer Claribel.

Union Street, Market Rasen in about 1900, looking up the street away from the Methodist Chapel. The River Rase runs through the town on its way to the Ancholme.

De Aston Grammar School, at Market Rasen, was opened in 1863 at a cost of £5,000 and named after Thomas De Aston, a medieval canon of Lincoln and Archdeacon of Stow. Old boys of this school include Cecil Jollands (former Chapter Clerk at Lincoln Cathedral), Peter Glover, who played rugby for England, and John Gladwin, whose group Amazing Blondel became well known in the '70s.

The last thing you would expect in the middle of the Lincolnshire Wolds is a motorcycle racing track. Cadwell Park, known throughout the world, was purchased by Mansfield Wilkinson in 1926 as a shooting estate. His son, Charles Wilkinson, saw its potential as a possible motorcycle circuit, and in 1934 the first track was laid. Of all the many famous names that have ridden at Cadwell, including Geoff Duke, John Surtees, Mike Hailwood, Phil Read, Barry Sheene, Roger Marshall and Wayne Gardner, probably the most memorable was Giacomo Agostini. It was not Agostini's favourite circuit, because it demanded much concentration and prevented him from going as fast as he could have liked.

Trafford's Stores of Alvingham has been one of the casualties of changes in rural life in recent decades. Despite being an established post office, this small family business has closed owing to the rigours of the twentieth-century trading, which is sad when you think that old Mr Trafford took his wares around by horse and cart at the turn of the century.

NORTH LINCOLNSHIRE
NOT HUMBERSIDE

About 4½ miles south-east of Barton lies the grand entrance to Thornton Abbey, the property of the Earls of Yarborough, in the scattered village of Thornton Curtis.

Grimsby once had a wonderful network of trams. This is Freeman Street, which eventually leads down to the docks, with the old tram lines clearly visible in the middle of the road.

By the end of the nineteenth century Grimsby had become the most important fishing port in the United Kingdom. This aerial view of the 1880s was taken from Grimsby Dock Tower, the brick masterpiece of architect James William Wild (1814–92).

There have been many fine upstanding Grimbarians but there have also been some dubious characters. One rogue who captured the public's imagination was Dod Osborne, who stole the seine-netter *Girl Pat* in 1936. When the boat was supposed to be fishing off the west coast of Scotland, Captain Osborne was secretly heading for Spain. He put in for supplies at the tiny Spanish port of Concubion and left with bills unpaid, then at the naval station of Dakar in French West Africa, before finally being cornered off British Guiana. The *Girl Pat* was then returned to England, touted around the English seaside resorts as a tourist attraction, and finally ended her days in the sunny Caribbean.

Even in the '30s, when this photograph was taken, there was plenty of work on the docks and in those days Britain used to export coal.

These days commercial traffic prefers nearby Immingham, which flourishes. The twentieth century has made Immingham what it is – a port with a deep-water dock on a landlocked harbour. This view of the graving dock, entrance lock and general offices was part of the GCR Publicity Department's advertising campaign, before the First World War.

Travelling along the tip of the county one encounters the three Killingholme lighthouses, of which these are two. Killingholme High Lighthouse (built in 1831 and enlarged in 1876), together with Killingholme Low Lighthouse (built in 1836), served as guides to shipping in the Humber.

At Barton-on-Humber there were celebrations for Mafeking Day, 1900. With flags flying and the keel built, work stopped for these shipbuilders and carpenters to enjoy the celebrations.

Barton-on-Humber was a port of considerable importance at one time. In fact, it was the biggest port on the Humber until Hull grew up across the estuary, taking away Barton's cargoes and shipbuilding industry. Now it is a little market town about a mile from the waterside but, since the Humber Bridge was erected (seen here under construction in the early 1970s), Barton's future may have been revived once more.

In the days before the First World War much emphasis was given to carpentry. It was taught in schools as a basic craft and because of this a whole host of joiners and craftsmen carpenters emerged, the like of which we will never see again. This is a woodwork class in Scunthorpe in 1905 depicting the value of good joints and the variations in seasoned wood. Note the vices on the ends of the benches.

St Peter's Church with Barton-on-Humber is one of the few Saxon towers left in England and has probably the best example. Incidentally, St Peter's Church is sometimes referred to as Old St Peter's.

Typical of Barton's old shops was Burton's fruit shop in King Street, seen here with Frank Burton (the son of J.W. Burton) standing in the doorway. The photograph was taken in 1923.

A diesel shunter at Barton railway station, 1963.

Originally built by the Corbett family in 1788 on the site of an earlier house, Elsham Hall has been added to and altered over the years. This photograph was taken in 1950. Members of the Elwes family of Elsham have included Gervase Elwes (singer), Simon Elwes (artist), Polly Elwes (TV presenter) and Dominic Elwes, whose antics hit the gossip columns in the 1960s. There is even an Elwes Street in Brigg.

Brigg was immortalised by Delius in his composition 'Brigg Fair'. Farmers would bring their weekly produce and beasts to market here. There is a fine selection of inns, such as the White Hart, the Brocklesby Ox and the Dying Gladiator.

It is here that the River Ancholme runs to the Humber, parallel with the Weir Dyke. Some of the warehouses that once lined this water's edge are still standing.

The small church of St John Evangelist lies in Bigby Street, built by W.A. Nicholson in 1842. Pevsner rather unfairly damned Brigg in his book on Lincolnshire by saying that 'a walk of Brigg is short and uneventful'!

Nearby Caistor church is set in the grounds of the old Roman camp with its own Roman well, still in use. These Edwardian children are on their way to attend their weekly Sunday School. Inside the church is a stained glass window in memory of the Kennington family, of which Eric Kennington (1880–1960), the First World War artist, was a member.

Caistor Grammar School, founded in 1631 by Francis Rawlinson, has a good reputation. This group was photographed in about 1860, when Anthony Bower was the headmaster. The most famous old boy of the school is Sir Henry Newbolt, the poet.

Princess Diana strolled along the banks of the Ancholme on 29 March 1988 in the company of the Mayor of Glanford, Mrs Violet Lockwood. The Princess was due to plant a commemorative tree.

Just to remind every schoolboy of the dangers of sloth, Caistor Union (the old workhouse) was in Kelsey Road.

Typical of Caistor's shops was William Shearsmith's in Chapel Street, photographed in 1905 by J. Wood. It was a provisions store, selling flour and barley meal together with boiled sweets and Sunlight soap.

When there was an event in Caistor everyone supported it. This was Queen Victoria's Golden Jubilee of 1897.

Of course the main event in the farming calendar was threshing time. This group of agricultural labourers was photographed near Caistor in about 1900 by Lacy & Clay.

Caistor boasted some industrious pastimes. Here, the Caistor Ladies' Needlework Society is on its annual outing to Pelham's Pillar, Brocklesby Park, *c.* 1890.

Pelham's Pillar. Excursions to Pelham's Pillar were still popular in the '20s. The pillar (138 ft high) commemorated the first Lord Yarborough's (Charles Anderson Pelham) planting of 1,352,700 trees on his North Lincolnshire estate. Two lions (one awake and one asleep) guard the base, as can be seen in this photograph of about 1925.

The other building at Great Limber in Brocklesby Park which attracts architecture buffs is the Mausoleum. This was also erected by Charles Anderson Pelham, following the death of his wife Sophia in 1786. It was designed by James Wyatt (1746–1813) in the Palladian style. This photograph was taken on 20 July 1868 by the Louth photo-grapher Joseph Willey.

Brocklesby Park, the Pelham family seat, has only survived because of architect Sir Reginald Blomfield's meticulous restoration after a fire gutted the building in 1898. The Brocklesby hounds make a wonderful subject in front of this stately building, reputed to have been modelled on Buckingham House. The wooden clock over the stable block was made by John Harrison (1693–1776), who invented the chronometer. It has always kept perfect time!

On the estate is this Memorial Arch, inscribed to the 2nd Earl of Yarborough in 1864 by his tenants and friends. The sum of £2,000 was collected to erect the arch at the west entrance to Brocklesby Park. It is no wonder that a later Earl of Yarborough wanted his estate to be included in Lincolnshire, rather than the newly formed County of Humberside. Thank goodness, now that North Lincolnshire has reverted back to its roots and the County of Humberside no longer exists, that these petty arguments can be forgotten and buried.

Another town that has had some bad press recently and has suffered as the butt of many a joke is Scunthorpe. Although described as a hamlet in the Domesday Book, it has outstripped its neighbouring villages of Frodingham, Crosby, Brumby and Ashby, and is currently a busy market and industrial town. These are the old Palace Theatre and post office.

One of the most fascinating shops was the Little Spec Shop at 95 High Street, Scunthorpe. It had branches at Market Rasen and Crowle and sold cameras too! Tony Jacklin, the golfer, was born in Scunthorpe as was the footballer Kevin Keegan.

The iron works at Frodingham pre-dated the now heavily industrialised Humber Bank, churning out an assortment of fumes, gases and sulphur. The Frodingham Iron Works was erected in 1867 by Joseph Cliff of Wortley but it was not until 1890 that the first metal was run off. This view of the North Iron Works was taken in about 1900.

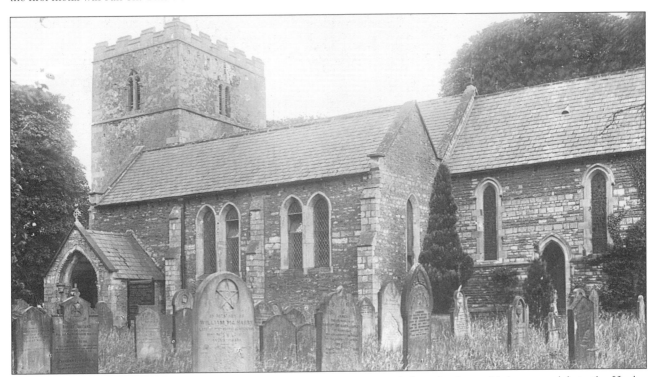

In contrast to the steelworks, Frodingham's old church of St Lawrence stands bravely alone with its memorials to the Healey family. In 1895 the Revd Edward Weigall was vicar here.

Just south of Frodingham, in the Isle of Axholme, is the small market town of Epworth. Samuel Wesley came here in 1696 as rector and here many of his nineteen children were born, including John Wesley, the father of Methodism, in 1703, and Charles Wesley, in 1708, who wrote over 600 hymns. Epworth's present rectory is not the Wesleys' original rectory, which was burned down in 1709 by an angry mob who objected to Samuel Wesley's political affiliations. John Wesley (1703–91) travelled 250,000 miles and preached 40,000 sermons – often in the open air. At first church doors were closed to him, but later on those same churches were too small to hold a fraction of the crowds that gathered to hear him. To commemorate the Wesleys and Methodists in general two chapels were built, of which this is one. Built in 1889 in memory of John Wesley and his brother Charles it is called the Wesley Memorial Chapel, while the other was built in 1860 in memory of Alexander Kilham (1762–98), founder of the New Connexion of Methodists, who was also born in Epworth; it is called the New Connexion Methodist Chapel.

One of the most remarkable features which takes place near Gainsborough is the tidal bore known as the Ægir, which runs along the Trent. Details of tides can be obtained through Gainsborough Tourist Office.

Brook's Mill, Epworth, was built in about 1800 and originally known as the White Mill. It was still working in the 1940s but after the sails were removed in 1962 it was derelict until 1982, when it was converted into a private house.

Just south of Gainsborough, in between Gainsborough and Lincoln, is the magnificent building of Stow church. Stow was the old cathedral in Lindsey in Saxon times, before Lincoln Cathedral was a twinkle in Bishop Remigius' eye.

On the subject of religion, back in Immingham is the granite stone which was taken from Plymouth Rock, Massachusetts, and erected in 1924 to mark the spot where some of the Pilgrim Brethren set sail for Holland in 1608; there was a further sailing in 1609. This memorial should not be confused with the other Pilgrim Fathers' memorial of Scotia Creek, Fishtoft, near Boston in Lincolnshire, which commemorated the 1607 sailing. All these emigrants assembled in Amsterdam in their search for religious freedom and settled in Leyden from 1609 to 1620 before making their historic voyage on the *Mayflower* in 1620.

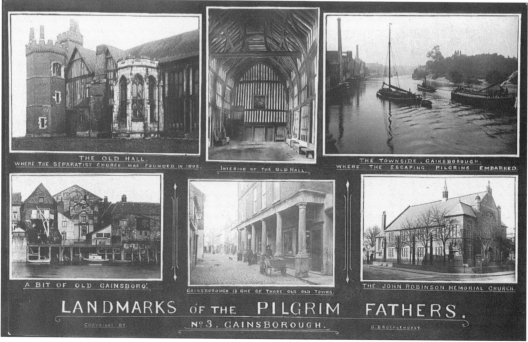

Gainsborough produced this postcard depicting The Old Hall, where the Separatist Church was founded in 1602. Simon Patrick, a former Bishop of Chichester and Ely, was born in Gainsborough in 1626, as was that memorable twentieth-century actress Dame Sybil Thorndike.

BOSTON &
THE FENS

Boston was known as Icanhoe until the Saxon Monk Botolph built his monastery here in AD 654. This monastery was demolished in AD 870, and no trace of it is left today. Icanhoe then became known as Botolphstowne, which was shortened over the years to Boston. This photograph was taken from the Grand Sluice Bridge.

Boston has always been a trading and commercial centre, more so in the fourteenth century than of late. During this time it has acquired the nickname of 'Capital of the Fens', and is dominated by the familiar 272½ ft high tower known as Boston Stump.

Boston Market Place, *c.* 1894, when William Mitchell was landlord of the Angel Hotel.

The prominent statue in the Market Place is of Herbert Ingram, founder of the *Illustrated London News* in 1842. He also represented Boston in Parliament but unfortunately drowned in an accident on Lake Michigan on 8 September 1860 at the age of forty-nine. He was one of Boston's most famous sons, and was also instrumental in bringing Boston its first supply of piped water.

Boston Dock is still an import/export centre. The timber vessel in this photograph has possibly been loaded a bit too enthusiastically, which accounts for its heavy list.

At first glance this looks a bit like the facsimile of HMS *Endeavour* which visited Boston Dock in 1997. It is in fact the *Ruby*, photographed in 1913.

The ferry that used to carry passengers over the Witham was at this point on the river in Boston. In the foreground is the steam tug *Privateer*.

The steamship *Bulldog* in about 1913, passing some of the many warehouses which only twenty years ago were derelict. Many have now been given a new lease of life by renovation work.

The stocks were preserved in Boston for many years although locals were convinced they were not preserved for long enough. This photograph was taken in about 1900.

Boston's old town bridge on the Witham, which was condemned in 1912, can be seen in the middle distance. It was demolished in 1913.

Boston's new town bridge under construction in June 1913.

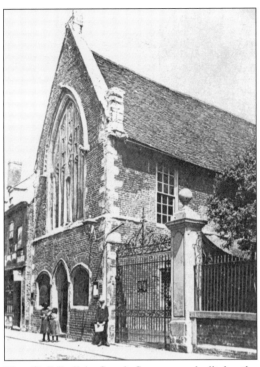

The Guildhall in South Street was built by the Guild of St Mary, and after the abolition of the Guilds it was used as a town hall for more than 300 years. In the basement are the cells in which the Pilgrim Fathers were imprisoned after their first attempt to leave England.

Probably the most unusual building in Boston is Shodfriars Hall, completely restored in 1874 by J. Oldrid Scott (architect) at a cost of £9,000. It replaced 'The Old House', leaving little if anything of the earlier building after restoration.

The quay, Boston, early twentieth-century.

Popular Boston views, c. 1930.

Looking down Bargate towards the Stump, with the post office on the right, *c.* 1910.

The 5th Boston Scout Group photographed at Swineshead Abbey in about 1914, when the scout mistress was Miss Hope Young.

Boston Grammar School was built in 1567 after being endowed by Queen Mary in 1554. The Headmaster in 1893 was Mr W. White, who had been appointed in 1887.

The old Wesleyan chapel gives us a clue to the influence which John Wesley had on Boston.

The Boston Wesleyan chapel was built in about 1911 after the original chapel burned down on 29 June 1909. Here we see men standing in the wreckage of the old chapel, which had been built in 1839.

The old Boston Cottage Hospital, built in 1871 from designs by W.H. Wheeler, had its own recreational grounds from 1874. It was a far cry from the new Pilgrim Hospital.

Landmarks in and around Boston included the old windmill at Stickford. Its four sails were removed in the 1960s because of their dangerous condition. Although derelict, there is a chance that this mill (dated 1820) might one day be restored, because internally the mill is complete.

Of the many farmhouses in the area is the unpretentious Coupledyke Hall in Frieston. It was once the seat of Sir Alexander de Cubbledick (1291–1334) who married Joan Huntingfield (heiress of Huntingfield Hall, West Wickham, Kent). The present farmhouse is built around the foundations of the old medieval hall.

At the nearby Marine Hotel on Freiston Shore, there was a wooden bridge to enable guests to walk straight on to the sea bank to view tides, marshland and birdlife; this stretch of waterlogged marsh has since become reclaimed land. When I last visited the Marine Hotel it was in a poor state of repair.

The windmill at Friskney (Toffs) did not fare too well either. Like so many other wooden-framed windmills, Stevenson's Mill was eventually demolished.

St Luke's Church, Stickney, had its porch rebuilt in 1887 by Bassett Smith, who also half rebuilt the tower in 1900. Then it stood for a considerable time like this until enough money was found and the tower was finally completed.

South of Boston is Holland Fen. A series of dykes protect this low-lying land from flooding.

Because Fenland soil is so fertile, root vegetables such as sugar beet, carrots, turnips, swedes and potatoes grow well. Here we see a group of potato pickers from Holbeach St John's in about 1905.

In this further photograph of potato pickers from Ferriby Sluice in about 1890, the women are wearing their Lincolnshire bonnets, once such a common sight. These bonnets were hand made and attractively gathered; they had a starch-stiffened 'poke' which served either to shade the face from constant sunshine on hot days or could be turned back on dull days.

These same bonnets were used when gleaning. This photograph was taken near Pinchbeck and the village church is in the background. The term gleaning means gathering together useful remnants of a crop from the field after harvesting.

Spalding is the last town on the River Welland before it reaches the Wash. This winter scene shows an old barge, typical of the many that once plied this stretch of water.

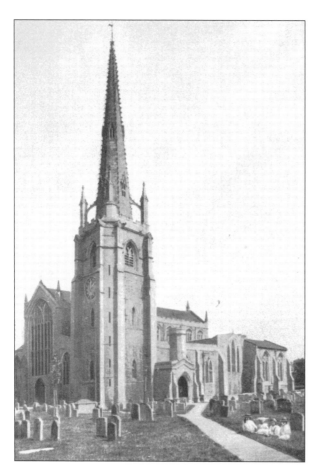

Spalding's crowning glory is St Mary and St Nicholas' Church. Although there was a church on this site from 1284, much of the present building owes its influence to the costly restoration of architect Sir Gilbert Scott in 1865, which left it with a fine hammerbeam roof.

The Fens can boast a fine collection of churches. This example of St Mary Magdalen, Fleet, near Holbeach, is unusual in that the steeple complete with spire is totally detached from the main body of the church. The late John Piper, artist, was fascinated by Lincolnshire churches and spent hours photographing and sketching them.

A farm labourer stooking, or stowking, on Cowbit Wash near Spalding. The photograph was taken in about 1890 and it is interesting to note that the bands going around the stooks are also made of corn stalks. No baling twine used here!

From one end of the county to the other. Here we see the Grimsby Port Master's annual staff picnic of 1931 to Crowland, a small ancient market town on the south-east side of Deeping Fen.

This unique triangular bridge spanned three streams formed by the River Welland and the Catwater Drain. Once these streams were filled in, the bridge (with its three semi-arches) was left as an interesting object of antiquity.

SOUTH LINCOLNSHIRE

Next door to Pinney's watchmaker's and jeweller's shop at 21 High Street, Stamford, was Smedley's poultry shop, seen here decked out with Christmas fare – a common practice in Victorian and Edwardian times.

On the way south of Lincoln, on the Grantham road, was Coleby Mill, which was a tall six-sailer. It was demolished in 1942 because of its proximity to the airfield and, since then, the remaining stump has been removed.

Sleaford derives its name from the River Slea. At the centre of the market town is the church of St Denis which contains probably the finest examples of window tracery in England. There are also several monuments to the Carre family, one of whom founded a grammar school in Sleaford.

About 5½ miles south-west of Sleaford is the handsome manor of Culverthorpe Hall, long the home of the Newtons, which passed by descent to Lt.-Col. G. Eyre in the last century. In the small church there are numerous monuments to the Newton family of Culverthorpe, the most peculiar being a marble slab in the floor to an infant son, who was dropped over the parapet of the house by a pet monkey in 1733!

The Bourne Corn Exchange and Public Hall (built in 1870) were put up on the site of the old post office at a cost of £1,200. William Cecil (1520–98), Lord Burghley, was born in Bourne as indeed was Charles Frederick Worth (1825–95), the French dress designer who founded Parisian *haute couture*. But the most remarkable was Robert Manning (or Robert de Brunne), who was credited with giving the English language its present shape.

One of the largest industries in Bourne was Mays, who dealt in woolstapling and fellmongering, malting, hides and chemical manures.

Folkingham square was, and still is, dominated by the Greyhound Inn, a reminder of its importance in coaching days. This magnificent Queen Anne brick hostelry of the late eighteenth century commands some breathtaking views of the surrounding countryside.

At the turn of the century C.A. Simpson was the carrier transporting goods between Bourne and Sleaford. At the foot of Castle Hill are the remains of the House of Correction, built in 1808.

Situated on the Bourne road is Corby, a pleasant market town which once had one of the largest annual sheep fairs in the country, held on the Monday before 11 October.

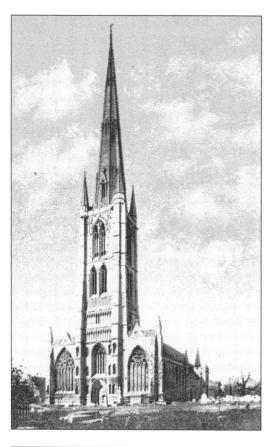

Grantham's crowning glory is the magnificent spire of St Wulfram's church which, like St James' spire in Louth or Boston Stump, or even Lincoln Cathedral, serves as a familiar landmark for miles around. However, it would be impossible to photograph it from this angle today because of the trees.

Like Lincoln, Grantham held house sales in Westgate and Cattle Market and had businesses which depended on the trade. This early twentieth-century advertisement for saddlery was placed by Wilkinson & Hawley's.

Chambers' millinery shop in the High Street, Grantham, also sold carpets, lino and soft furnishings.

There are many fine houses around Grantham, including Harlaxton and Belton House. The author's favourite is Stoke Hall, seen here in about 1905.

The size of the sheep fairs in Stamford can be seen in this photograph. There was only enough room for prospective purchasers and pedestrians to walk beside the pens on narrow pavements.

Although there are some sheep left in Lincolnshire, the numbers have diminished dramatically since the Second World War. Here we see Mr Brown and his collie at the World Ploughing Championships in 1984 which were held in Lincolnshire.

Stamford is well known for Burghley House, Daniel Lambert and the George Hotel. Here we see the George draped in creeper in about 1910; this has since been removed.

Browne's Hospital in Broad Street, Stamford, was founded in 1483 by William Browne, a wealthy wool merchant (six times Alderman of Stamford and a Sheriff of Rutland). Although called a hospital, it was more along the lines of a hospice or residential home. It was designed to take twelve men and was run by a Warden and his Confrater.

Stamford is situated on the Welland, one of the four rivers running into the Wash – the Welland, the Witham, the Nene and the Ouse. It made a perfect setting for the BBC's 1990s production of *Middlemarch*. This photograph shows St Paul's Street, *c.* 1930.

High Street, St Martin's and St Mary's Hill, Stamford, *c.* 1930. The old sign advertising the George Hotel still straddles the street despite the fact that pantechnicons and high-sided lorries now pass this way.

The ruins of the ancient Benedictine abbey at Crowland, 1954. Spelt Croyland in times past, the abbey was built in the eighth century by King Aethelbald, in memory of St Guthlac, and was finally destroyed during the dissolution of the monasteries by Henry VIII in the 1540s.

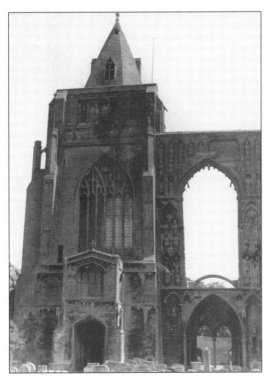

Algarkirk has one of the finest churches in Fenland. Seen here in 1958, it was restored in 1850 by R.C. Carpenter. The church encompasses the Victorian sympathy with medieval design. Woad – a plant used to make blue dye – was still cultivated in the area until about 1930 and the woad mill survives.

ACKNOWLEDGEMENTS

There are numerous people whom I must thank for helping me to prepare this volume, in particular Geoffrey Roe, Michael Surr, Brian Howe, Stephen Clarke, the late Cecil Simpson, Janet Longden, David Elliott, Bernard Hallgath, John Neilson, Peter Craig, Chris Volley, Cecil Jollands, Rowland Hall, Charles Smith, Ben Jacklin, the late James Baildom, Peter Chapman, Graham Perkins, Peter Chambers and John Turner.

INDEX